THE WISDOM

of the

HINDU GURUS

TIMOTHY FREKE

℔

First published in 1998 by Journey Editions, an imprint of
Periplus Editions (HK) Ltd., with editorial offices at
153 Milk Street, Boston, Massachusetts 02109.

Distributed by:
USA
Charles E. Tuttle Co., Inc. RR 1 Box 231-5
North Clarendon, VT 05759
Tel.: (802) 773-8930 Fax.: (802) 773-6993

Japan
Tuttle Shokai Ltd. 1-21-13, Seki
Tama-ku, Kawasaki-shi
Kanagawa-ken 214
Japan
Tel.: (044) 833-0225 Fax.: (044) 822-0413

Southeast Asia
Berkeley Books Pte. Ltd. 5 Little Road #08-01
Singapore 536983
Tel.: (65) 280-3320 Fax.: (65) 280-6290

ISBN 1-885203-56-X
The Catalog Card Number is on file with
the Library of Congress

Printed in Hong Kong

CONTENTS

The Tree of Knowledge

............X............

India may be poor materially, but she has always been rich with enlightened spiritual teachers, known as "gurus." The name "guru" means "one who leads from darkness to light." Gurus guide their followers through the spiritual journey, along a route they themselves have successfully traversed, to the goal of awakening that they have already reached. They are living proof of the truth of their teachings. With some of India's greatest gurus as our guides, this book explores the depths of Mother India's spiritual knowledge. The gurus lead us on a mystical journey from separation to unity, from ignorance to self-realization, from selfishness to service, from a troubled mind to an open heart; from illusion to love.

The various Hindu spiritual paths, known as "yogas," are different routes to the same Truth. "Yoga" means "union," and its goal is oneness with God. The two most important yogas are gnana yoga and bhakti yoga – the way of the head and the way of the heart. Through philosophy and meditation, gnanis come to realize that their personal self is merely an illusion

caused by thoughts in the mind and that in reality everything is One. Bhaktas lose themselves in all-consuming ecstatic devotion to God, until all that exists is the love-play between God and his devotee. Most gurus teach a combination of gnana yoga and bhakti yoga, often accompanied by karma yoga. Through service to others, karma yogis transform their lives into love-in-action and become instruments of God's will. The end of all yogas is the same realization. We are not transitory individuals. We are immortal and divine. We are one with God who is the supreme, permanent, and only reality.

1 Santana Dharma

························◈························

Hinduism is a broad religion, resplendent with many colorful gods and goddesses. However, these deities are all seen as embodying different aspects of the one supreme God. There is, therefore, no conflict between those that worship God in different disguises and with different names. Hinduism points beyond particular religious dogmas and practices to a direct experience of God. It is a remarkably tolerant religion that recognizes that all spiritual paths are different routes up the same mountain. The great Hindu gurus do not see themselves as teaching Hinduism, but the all-embracing "Santana Dharma" – "The Eternal Teachings of the Truth."

> **"** That which we call the Hindu religion
> is really the eternal religion
> because it embraces all others. **"**
>
> SRI AUROBINDO

Truth is One and the learned call it by many names.

RIG VEDA

“ Religions are different roads converging on the same point. What does it matter that we take different roads so long as we reach the same goal? I believe that all religions of the world are true more or less. I say "more or less" because I believe that everything the human hand touches, by reason of the very fact that human beings are imperfect, becomes imperfect. ”

MAHATMA GANDHI

" Three men went into the jungle on different occasions and saw a chameleon. "A chameleon is red," said the first man. "No a chameleon is green," said the second man. "Nonsense, a chameleon is brown," said the the third man. Those who disagree about the nature of God are like these three men. "

HINDU TEACHING STORY

It is better to see God in everything than to try and figure it out.

NEEM KAROLI BABA

" A king asked a sage to explain the Truth. In response the sage asked the king how he would convey the taste of a mango to someone who had never eaten anything sweet. No matter how hard the king tried, he could not adequately describe the flavor of the fruit, and, in frustration, he demanded of the sage "Tell me then, how would you describe it?" The sage picked up a mango and handed it to the king saying "This is very sweet. Try eating it!" "

HINDU TEACHING STORY

What can be gained by thinking about the scriptures? What fools! They think themselves to death with information about the path, but never take the plunge!

RAMAKRISHNA

Truth is no theory, no speculative system of philosophy, no intellectual insight. Truth is exact correspondence with reality. For man, truth is the unshakeable knowledge of his real nature, his Self.

PARAMHANSA YOGANANDA

66 Illness is not cured by saying the word "medicine,"
but by taking medicine. Enlightenment is not
achieved by repeating the word "God" but by
directly experiencing God.

Talk as much philosophy as you like,
worship as many gods as you please,
observe ceremonies and sing devotional hymns,
but liberation will never come, even after a hundred
aeons, without realizing the Oneness. 99

SANKARA

*All those who walk with God
reach their destination.*

SAI BABA

66 A saint saw that hunters were laying nets to catch
birds and baiting them with bread, so he taught
a parrot to fly around the jungle squawking
"Don't eat the bread or you'll get caught! Don't eat
the bread!" The other birds heard his message
and avoided the bread, but the parrot was only
repeating what the saint had taught him and didn't
understand what he was saying. When all the other
birds had flown away he flew down to eat the
bread and was caught by the hunter's net. 99

HINDU TEACHING STORY

66 You seek too much information
and not enough transformation. 99

SAI BABA

66 The supreme truth is established by total silence,
not logical discussion and argument.

He alone sees the truth who sees the
universe without the intervention of the mind, and
therefore without the notion of a universe. 99

MAHARAMAYANA

*Self-knowledge cannot be gained until
everything is renounced. When all points of
view are abandoned, what remains is the
Self. Even in the world you do not get what
you desire until all obstacles are removed.
This is even more true of self-knowledge.*

MAHARAMAYANA

*One cannot but laugh and even be
apparently irreverent when confronted by
the fantastic super structure of superstition
and mystery that has been built on and
around the basic simplicity that TRUTH is!*

RAMESH BALSEKAR

II Brahman

❖

Brahman is the supreme God, the ineffable and indescribable oneness of all things. Within sentient beings he appears as the "Atman," the conscious Self, the sense of "I am," pure Consciousness. In the world He manifests as everything that is perceived by the senses. He is the great sea of Being from which all that exists originates and returns. All forms of separateness are in reality "maya" – an illusion. Only the oneness of Brahman ultimately exists. Brahman is all and does all. The realization of the all-pervading reality of Brahman is the highest goal of Hinduism.

> ❝ There is no one here
> except the Lord of Love.
> Only He exists.
> In truth, He alone is. ❞
>
> MUNDAKA UPANISHAD

*It is you that pervades this universe,
and this universe exists in you.
Your true nature is pure Consciousness.
Don't be small-minded.*

ASHTAVAKRA GITA

> 66 A poor devotee points to the sky and says,
> "God is up there."
> An average devotee says,
> "God dwells in the heart as the Inner Master."
> The best devotee says, "God alone is and everything
> I perceive is a form of God." 99

RAMAKRISHNA

*There exists something that
cannot be described.*

MAHARAMAYANA

The moon is one, but on agitated
water it produces many reflections.
Similarly ultimate reality is one,
yet it appears to be many in a mind
agitated by thoughts.

MAHARAMAYANA

The ultimate Consciousness
is always present everywhere.
It is beyond space and time,
with no before or after.
It is undeniable and obvious.
So what can be said about it?

ABHINAVAGUPTA

Meditate and realize that this world
is full of the presence of God.

SHVETASHVATARA UPANISHAD

To see God everywhere
you have to have special eyes,
otherwise you cannot bear the shock.

NEEM KAROLI BABA

That which cannot be comprehended
by the mind,
but by which the mind comprehends;
that which encompasses the mind –
know that to be Brahman.

That which cannot be seen by the eyes,
but by which the eyes see –
know that to be Brahman.

KENA UPANISHAD

God is Consciousness that pervades
the entire universe of the living
and the non-living.

RAMAKRISHNA

66 The Vedas compare creation to a spider's web,
that the spider creates and then lies within.
God is both the container of the universe
and what is contained in it. 99

RAMAKRISHNA

66 Brahman creates the game of life
by breaking Himself into parts that undergo
transformation and extinction.
Yet while he takes on all the roles required
by the game, He also always remains free of
the game and intact as Brahman. 99

ABHINAVAGUPTA

The same undivided and indivisible space
is outside and inside of a thousand pots.
Likewise the Self pervades all beings.

MAHARAMAYANA

Learn to look with an equal eye upon all
things, seeing the one Self in all.

SRIMAD BHAGAVATAM

> 66 Brahman is the Self hidden in everyone.
> He is only obvious to those who,
> minds focused one-pointedly on the Lord of Love,
> nurture intuitive knowledge.
> Meditation leads them deeper into consciousness,
> passing from the world to thoughts,
> and beyond thoughts to the wisdom of the Self. 99

KATHA UPANISHAD

> 66 My mind fell like a hailstone
> into the vast expanse of Brahman's ocean.
> Touching one drop of it,
> I melted away and became one with Brahman.
> This is wonderful indeed!
> Here is the ocean of Brahman,
> full of endless joy.
> How can I accept or reject anything?
> Is there anything apart or distinct from Brahman?
> Now, finally and clearly, I know that I am the Atman,
> whose nature is eternal joy.
> I see nothing. I hear nothing.
> I know nothing that is separate from me. 99

SANKARA

III Gnana Yoga

......................◈......................

Gnana Yoga – the path of knowledge – teaches that the external world of separate things is an illusion. This includes our sense of being a person, with a distinct identity and will. All separateness is only the product of thoughts in the mind. When the mind is still, the oneness of Brahman is revealed. The mortal person that we take ourselves to be is seen as just a passing phenomenon like everything else. This ego-self masks our essential identity which is the immortal "Atman" – the Self that is conscious through all sentient beings. This true Self is identical with Brahman. Ultimately we are all God.

The Self exists both inside
and outside of the physical body,
just like an image exists within
and outside the mirror.

ASHTAVAKRA GITA

66 To everyone of us there must come a time when the
whole universe will be found to have been a dream,
when we find the soul is infinitely better than
the surroundings. It is only a question of time,
and time is nothing in the infinite. 99

SAI BABA

His divine power creates
this magic show
of name and form and you and me;
casting a spell of pleasure and pain.

SHVETASHVATARA UPANISHAD

The mind is an object of perception
like the external world.
The Atman, the real seer,
remains unknown.

PANTANJALI

66 The stupid man looks at his body and says,
"This is I." The more learned thinks, "This is I" of his
personality. But the wise man knows the true Self,
saying, "I am the Eternal." He is individual, though
without separateness. He has dissolved the
"I" in Pure Consciousness.

Liberation cannot be achieved except through
perceiving the identity of the individual spirit
with the Universal Spirit. Atman and Brahman
are identical. Their essence is pure Consciousness. 99

SANKARA

66 The ego is like a thin patch of cloud
that prevents the sun being seen.
If, by the guru's grace, it disperses,
then one can see God.

The ego is like a stick dividing water into two.
It creates the impression
that you are one and I am another.
When the ego vanishes you will realize
that Brahman is your own inner consciousness. 99

RAMAKRISHNA

The ego and the Self
dwell as intimate friends in the same body,
like two golden birds perched in the same tree.
The ego eats the sweet and sour fruits of the tree,
while the Self looks on detached.
For as long as you identify with the ego,
you will feel joy and sorrow.
But if you know you are the Self, the Lord of Life,
you will be free from suffering;
the supreme source of light;
the supreme source of love.
You will transcend duality
and live in a state of Oneness.

MUNDAKA UPANISHAD

The Atman is the witness
of the mind and its workings.

SANKARA

There is only one state. When corrupted
and tainted by self-identification, it is
known as an individual. When merely
tinted by the sense of presence, of
animated consciousness, it is the
impersonal witnessing. When it remains in
its pristine purity, untainted and untinted
in primal repose, it is the Absolute.

RAMESH BALSEKAR

If you detach yourself from identification
with the body and remain relaxed in
and as Consciousness, you will, this very
moment, be happy, at peace, free from
bondage.

ASHTAVAKRA GITA

" The Atman is the witness-consciousness that
experiences the action, the actor, and the world of
separate things. It is like a light that illuminates
everything in a theater, revealing the master of
ceremonies, the guests, and the dancers with complete
impartiality. Even when they all depart,
the light shines to reveal their absence.

In this example, the master of ceremonies is the ego,
the guests are the objects of the senses, the dancers are
thoughts in the mind, and the light that reveals them is
the witnessing-consciousness. The light reveals all, just
as the witness-consciousness reveals the external world
of objects and the internal world
of subjective experience. "

PANCHADASHI

*Through self-effort and self-knowledge make the
mind no-mind. Let infinite Consciousness swallow
the finite mind, and then go beyond everything.*

*If you could give up thoughts, you will right here
and now attain the realization of oneness with all.*

*Don't think about ideas such as bondage and
liberation, simply abandon all craving and
through wisdom and dispassion bring about the
cessation of the mind. Even if the wish "may I be
liberated" arises, the mind will come back to life.*

MAHARAMAYANA

The eradication of the craving for personal separateness is Liberation.

SANKARA

66 The Lord is not to be worshiped with material things.
but with one's own consciousness.
Don't wave lights and incense. or offer flowers and
food. He is found effortlessly when worshiped through
self-realization alone. The continuous and unbroken
awareness of the indwelling presence, the inner light of
consciousness. is the supreme meditation and devotion.
Whatever you are doing. seeing. hearing. touching.
smelling. eating. or saying. realize your essential nature
as pure Consciousness. This is the way to liberation. 99

MAHARAMAYANA

*Liberation is only being rid
of the idea that there is anyone
who needs liberation.*

RAMESH BALSEKAR

> *The no-mind state is not the vacancy*
> *of idiocy but the most supremely alert*
> *intelligence, undistracted by*
> *extraneous thought.*
>
> RAMESH BALSEKAR

“ Enlightenment is merely an impersonal happening.
We give it the taint of personal achievement.
Therefore the question arises, "What is an enlightened
being like?" There is no such thing as an enlightened
person. Enlightenment is merely another event.
There is a flood, a fire, an earthquake;
there is enlightenment, just one happening in the whole
process, all part of the phenomenal process. ”

RAMESH BALSEKAR

> *All is God. Thoughts,*
> *desires are all God. Everything*
> *comes from God.*
>
> SAI BABA

If you would swim
on the bosom
of the ocean of Truth,
you must reduce
yourself to a zero.

MAHATMA GANDHI

Bodies come and go
like clothes.

SANKARA

*Having realized his own self as
the Self a person becomes selfless.*

MAITRAYANA UPANISHAD

*One cannot see God as long
as one feels "I am the doer."*

*Fully awakened souls are beyond
virtue and vice.
They realize that it is God
who does everything.*

RAMAKRISHNA

*Whatever decision we think
we are making
is actually being made for us,
because the decision is the end result
of a thought and we have no control
over the arising of the thought.*

RAMESH BALSEKAR

❝ If a man considers that he is born, he cannot avoid the fear of death. Let him find out if he has been born or if the Self has any birth. He will discover that the Self always exists, that the body that is born resolves itself into thought and that the emergence of thought is the root of all mischief. Find from where thoughts emerge. Then you will be able to abide in the ever-present inmost Self and be free from the idea of birth or the fear of death. ❞

RAMANA MAHARSHI

❝ You have squeezed yourself into the span of a lifetime and the volume of a body, and thus created the innumerable conflicts of life and death. Have your being outside this body of birth and death and all your problems will be solved. They exist because you believe yourself born to die. Undeceive yourself and be free. You are not a person. ❞

SRI NISARGADATTA MAHARAJ

As long as there is a "who"
asking the questions,
that "who" will continue
to remain puzzled.

RAMESH BALSEKAR

Self is only "Being," not being
this or that.
It is simple Being,
and there is an end of ignorance.

RAMANA MAHARSHI

Death is not the extinguishing
of the light,
but the blowing out of the candle
because the dawn has come.

RABINDRANATH TAGORE

The supreme Self
is unborn and undying.

ATMA UPANISHAD

Just as rivers flow from east and west
to merge with the one sea,
forgetting that they were ever separate rivers,
so all beings lose their separateness
when they eventually merge into pure Being.

CHANDOGYA UPANISHAD

IV Bhakti Yoga

⋯⋯⋯❖⋯⋯⋯

Bhakti yoga – the path of devotion – emphasizes losing the self in love for God. Devotees relate to God in an intimate and personal way as their Beloved. This is difficult with a purely impersonal and ineffable God, so Brahman is seen as manifesting in the many Hindu gods and goddesses that may be approached in a more personal way. The guru, who has transcended the illusion of being a separate self, is also seen as an embodiment of God and is worshiped as such. In ecstatic devotion bhaktas replace all their many desires with the one all-consuming desire for communion with God.

> 66 The way of devotion is as good as the way
> of knowledge. But as long as God keeps
> the feeling of ego in us, it is easier
> to follow the path of devotion. 99
>
> RAMAKRISHNA

The intense desire for God-realization is itself the way to it.

SRI ANANDAMAYI MM

❝ The guru is the Lord himself. To worship
the guru is to worship the Lord. Why should the Lord
choose to manifest through the guru? Why should he
not act directly? God is really all-pervading, above the
mind, without features, imperishable, and infinite.
How can such a one be worshiped? That is why,
out of compassion for his creatures, He takes the form
of the guru. The guru is the supreme God enclosed in
human skin. He walks the earth, concealed,
bestowing grace on his disciples. ❞

KULARNAVA TANTRA

*The Gnani wants to
become Brahman,
but the bhakta wants to taste the
sweetness, not be the sugar.*

RAMAKRISHNA

*The guru is the formless Self
within each one of us. He may
appear as a body to guide us,
but that is only his disguise.*

RAMANA MAHARSHI

*If all the land were turned to paper
and all the seas turned to ink,
and all the forests into pens
to write with,
they would still not suffice
to describe the greatness of the guru.*

KABIR

> 66 He who loves Me is made pure;
> his heart melts in joy.
> He rises to transcendental consciousness
> by rousing his higher emotions.
> Tears of joy flow from his eyes,
> his hair stands on end,
> his heart melts in love.
> The bliss in that state is so intense
> that forgetful of himself and his surroundings,
> he sometimes weeps profusely,
> or laughs, or sings, or dances.
> Such a devotee is a purifying influence
> upon the whole universe. 99

SRIMAD BHAGAVATAM

> 66 Imagine Brahman as a sea without shores.
> Through the cooling love of the bhakta some of the
> water becomes frozen into blocks of ice. Now and then,
> God assumes a form and reveals Himself to his lovers
> as a Person. But when the sun of Knowledge rises,
> the blocks of ice melt away and God is without form,
> no more a Person. He is beyond description.
> Who could describe Him? Anyone who tries
> disappears, unable to find his "I" any more. 99

RAMAKRISHNA

46

The world calls me mad. I am mad. You are
mad. The world is mad. Who is not mad?
Still these madmen call me mad. Some are
mad after name and fame. Some are mad
after money. Some are mad after flesh.
But blessed is he who is mad after God.
Such a madman am I!

RANG AVADHUT

I wait for Him to come down the road.
If he isn't coming, I ache and waste away.
If he is late, I pine and grow thin.
O mother, if he doesn't come tonight,
I'll be like a lovebird with no one to love.

MAHADEVI

Oh my heart! The Supreme Spirit,
the Great Master, is near you.
Wake up! Wake up!
Run to the feet of your Beloved,
for your Lord is here.
You have slept for untold ages,
this morning will you not awake?

~ KABIR

> When you are with someone you love very much,
> you can talk and it is pleasant, but the reality is not
> in the conversation. It is in simply being together.
> Meditation is the highest form of prayer. In it you are
> so close to God that you don't need to say a thing
> – it is just great to be together.

SWAMI CHETANANDA

> People weep for their spouses, their children,
> and their wealth, but who weeps for God?
> While a child is engrossed with its toys its mother
> attends to her household duties, but when the child
> throws the toys aside and screams for its mother,
> then the mother puts down her cooking pot
> and takes the child in her arms.

RAMAKRISHNA

Dark One, hear me, I am mad with visions.
Eaten up by separation,
I wander from place to place
covered in ash and clothed in skins.
My body is wasting all because of you.
Distraught and desperate,
I go from forest to forest.
Immortal and Unborn One, visit your beggar.
Extinguish her pain with your
pleasurable touch.
Mira says: "End this coming and going
Let me forever embrace your sweet feet."

MIRABAI

66 Someone who practices only bhakti yoga is like a blind
man who cannot see where to go, and in his enthusiasm
wanders off in the wrong direction. Someone who practices
only gnana yoga, on the other hand, is like a lame man
who can see the distant destination but, because his
knowledge remains only theoretical, makes no progress
towards it. However, if the love and energy of the bhakta
is combined with the wisdom and discrimination of the
gnani, seekers are sure to reach their destination. 99

HINDU TEACHING STORY

v Karma Yoga

........⬦........

Karma yoga – the path of action – emphasizes overcoming the self through selfless service. Karma yogis abandon the endless search for fulfilment of their personal desires and live in the world as servants of God. Karma yoga is more than developing the desire to do good, it is the transcendence of desire altogether. Those on this path completely surrender themselves to God and accept whatever His will decrees. They act from love and compassion for all beings, but without any attachment to the results of their actions. More than this, ultimately they realize that in reality they do nothing, for all actions come from God.

> ❝ A superior being does not render evil for evil.
> Never harm the wicked or the good or even criminals
> meriting death. A noble soul is always compassionate,
> even toward those who enjoy injuring others
> or who are actually committing cruel deeds
> – for who is without fault? ❞

RAMAYANA

Love is the strongest medicine.

NEEM KAROLI BABA

Can't you see it's all perfect?!

NEEM KAROLI BABA

66 God demands nothing less than complete
self surrender as the price of the only real freedom
worth having. And, when we lose ourselves,
we immediately find ourselves in the service
of all that lives.
It becomes our joy and recreation.
We are a new person, never weary
of spending ourselves in the service of God's creation. 99

MAHATMA GANDHI

STUDENT:
"How can I become enlightened?"

NEEM KAROLI BABA:
"Feed people."

66 Those who seek their own pleasure and ignore
the needs of others have wasted their lives.

Strive constantly to serve the welfare of the world;
by devotion to selfless work one attains
the supreme goal of life. 99

BHAGAVAD GITA

Love is selflessness,
– self is lovelessness.

SAI BABA.

Do not judge others, for when another
is judged you yourself are condemned.

SAI BABA

Before you speak, ask yourself,
is it kind, is it necessary,
is it true, does it improve on the silence?

SAI BABA

The individual "I" exists for as long
as there is desire for pleasure.

MAHARAMAYANA

66 Inwardly be free of all hopes and desires,
but outwardly do what needs to be done.
Without hopes in your heart, live as if you were full of
hopes. Live with your heart now cool and now warm,
just like everyone else. Inwardly give up the idea
"I am the doer," yet outwardly engage in all activities.
This is how to live in the world, completely free
from the least trace of ego. 99

MAHARAMAYANA

*Everything has to be the way
it is and could not possibly be
any other way.*

MAHARAMAYANA

66 No worldly delight is comparable to the delight
that will fill your heart when you completely
abandon all hopes and desires. 99

MAHARAMAYANA

The whole universe is your home.
All are your family.

NEEM KAROLI BABA

The characteristic of ignorant people
is that they strive to be other
than they are.

MAHARAMAYANA

Through selfless service, you will always
be fruitful and find fulfilment.
This is the promise of the Creator.

BHAGAVAD GITA

Love all, serve all.

SAI BABA

Those who realize the Self are always satisfied.
Having found the source of joy and fulfilment
they no longer seek happiness from the
external world. They have nothing to gain
or lose by any action; neither people
nor things can affect their security.

BHAGAVAD GITA

66 All our desire for the fruits of life are caused by a
feeling of emptiness. Once we are genuinely full,
what other fruits would we desire? 99

ABHINAVAGUPTA

66 Do all your duties, but keep your mind on God.
Serve your wife, children, father, and mother, and treat
them as if they are very dear to you,but know in your
heart that they do not belong to you. 99

RAMAKRISHNA

*Remember the whole thing is just a play
and the Lord has assigned you a part. Act
your part well; there all your duty ends.
He has designed the play and he enjoys it.*

SAI BABA

*Spontaneous, true action happens
naturally when there is no "you"
checking whether the action conforms
to your idea of what is best for you.*

RAMESH BALSEKAR

*Those whose spiritual awareness has been
awakened never make a false move.
They don't have to avoid evil. They are
so replete with love that whatever they
do is a good action. They are fully
conscious that they are not the doer of
their actions, but only servants of God.*

RAMAKRISHNA

The publishers would like to thank the following for the use of pictures:

e.t. archive: pp. 28, 41, 48
Vanessa Fletcher: pp. 3, 9, 11, 13, 14, 15, 17, 19, 20, 23, 24, 27, 31,
33, 34, 37, 39, 43, 44, 47, 50, 57, 58